The
Hawkhurst
Branch l

Peter A. Har(

GW00758891

R class 0-4-4T No.31675 with the branch train at Hawkhurst Station. September 22nd 1951.
R.F.Roberts

Published by Peter A. Harding,
"Mossgiel", Bagshot Road, Knaphill,
Woking, Surrey GU21 2SG.

ISBN 0 9523458 3 8

First published 1982
Revised edition 1998

Contents

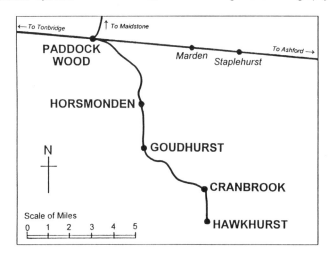

An unidentified H class 0-4-4T arriving at Cranbrook Station with the branch train for Hawkhurst. August 6th 1956.
H.Davies

Introduction

For a small country branch line, the Hawkhurst branch had everything that the rural railway enthusiast finds hard to resist. The single track wound its way for 11½ miles through delightful scenery with numerous hop gardens, orchards, woods, narrow valleys, hills, two short tunnels, oast-houses and period Wealden farm buildings to form the background,

The tank engines and pull-and-push sets of two carriages would climb the steeply graded line, through the Wealden hills, arriving exhausted by the effort at the terminus, over a mile north of Hawkhurst, on the border of Kent and Sussex.

The branch is probably best remembered for its association with the hop-pickers. They would leave their London homes at the end of each August, and descend on the hutments of the Kentish hop gardens, providing casual labour for a three week "working holiday" gathering the crops. Whole families would pick hops, live in "hopper huts" (a type of corrugated shed) and would take over the local villages during the evenings and weekends.

The Hawkhurst branch played a big part in bringing the hop-pickers. But when in the late 1950's, due to paid holidays and rising living standards, the hop-pickers stopped coming, and those that did came by road, the local railway was reaching the end of its life.

Today, hops are picked by mechanical pickers and a few students, and like the branch line to Hawkhurst, the hop-pickers are just a fading memory. I hope that those readers who remember the branch will, by reading this booklet, be able to re-live some happy times. And those who never saw it during its working life will be able to capture at least some of its charm and character.

H class 0-4-4T No.31518 heads the branch train for Hawkhurst, having just left the main line near Paddock Wood. Note the unusual Paddock Wood distant signal which was a standard upper quadrant bolted to a sawn-off telegraph pole. This replaced the original far more elegant wooden-posted signal which was taken down in the late 1950's.   B.R.Hart Collection

History of the Line

The main line of the South Eastern Railway (SER) which left the joint line of the London, Brighton & South Coast Railway (LBSCR) at Redhill, went through Tonbridge, Headcorn and Ashford to Folkestone, and was opened in stages during 1842 and 1843. A branch from Tonbridge to Tunbridge Wells was opened in 1845, and later extended via Robertsbridge to Hastings during 1851 and 1852. There it met the Hastings to Ashford line which was opened in 1851.

These lines now formed a triangle which enclosed a large agricultural area of Kent and East Sussex, well known for its hops and fruit, yet left small towns and villages like Cranbrook, Goudhurst, Hawkhurst and Tenterden off the railway map. Unfortunately this area embraced the Weald with its high ridges and deep valleys and was generally regarded as unsuitable terrain for the development of railways.

The SER was never very interested in developing local lines, and preferred to wait for a branch to be built with local money, then step in and purchase it at a low price when it failed to live up to expectations. The only time they showed concern was when their deadly rivals the London, Chatham & Dover Railway (LCDR) seemed likely to push their way into what the SER considered their area. Schemes which were put forward but failed to reach the statute book, were from Headcorn to Rye in 1844, and Paddock Wood to Rye Harbour Direct (with nominal SER support) in 1845. A line was projected from Headcorn to Tenterden via Cranbrook in 1855, but this proposal also came to nothing. Plans for a line from Marden to Cranbrook via Goudhurst in 1857 met a similar fate.

The next proposal for the area was put forward in 1864 by the Weald of Kent Railway for a line to run from Paddock Wood to Hythe by way of Cranbrook and Tenterden. Powers were obtained but still nothing came of it.

With the financial collapse of the LCDR in 1866, the SER felt no need to occupy the district as a defensive measure and was even able to oppose other expansive ideas.

In 1872 a modest scheme for a roadside tramway from Headcorn to Tenterden got no further, it seems, than a public meeting.

In 1877 the Cranbrook & Paddock Wood Railway was incorporated to build the northern part of the Weald of Kent Railway and obtained powers on August 8th of that year, for a line between Paddock Wood and Cranbrook.

Financial support for the company was to come from local residents, who appropriately chose a bunch of hops for the company seal, but at the half-yearly meeting on April 28th 1878, only £11,000 had been subscribed. It was stated that when £25,000 had been subscribed in the district, construction would begin, and that the SER would then contribute £25,000, and would provide another £25,000 on similar terms. It was also deemed that the railway would be constructed as an ordinary single track. In October 1878 the SER suggested that money could be saved by altering the position of Cranbrook Station.

Provisional work began in February 1879, but quickly came to a halt when local money was still not forthcoming and the SER showed little interest when approached. Even so, the promoters obtained a second Act on July 12th 1882 for a 1½ mile extension from Hartley to Hawkhurst. The original plan was for the line to run through Hartley into Cranbrook, hence the title of the company. Unfortunately, several landowners demanded too much money so it was decided to deviate the line from Hartley (which would become Cranbrook Station) to Hawkhurst. It now seemed clear that without SER support, nothing would be done. Later in the same year the SER stepped in, probably stimulated by the competitive policy of the LCDR who had again become a dangerous rival.

A lack of capital still delayed construction and between 1884 and 1890 further extensions of time were granted and re-routing of the line sanctioned. By September 1890, the Cranbrook & Paddock Wood Railway board of directors consisted of the following:-
The Hon. Alfred Erskine Gathorne-Hardy M.P. (Chairman), Captain Francis Pavy (Deputy Chairman), The Right Hon. Lord Brabourne, The Hon. James M.O. Bying, Philip B. Beresford-Hope and Alfred Mellor Watkin (son of the SER Chairman Sir Edward Watkin). Board meetings were held in London at either the Charing Cross Hotel, Cannon Street Hotel or London Bridge Station.

Edward P. Seaton

The engineer appointed to supervise the construction of the line was Edward P.Seaton who was connected to the Metropolitan Railway at Neasden, where he acted as an independent consultant.

The surprising choice of resident engineer was the 22 year old Holman Fred Stephens who, like Edward Seaton, was at that time also connected to the Metropolitan Railway at Neasden Works. He had just completed his education and training with some practical experience in their workshops and locomotive department, under Mr.J.J.Hanbury, who was resident engineer and locomotive superintendent to the Metropolitan Railway. The choice of Stephens was more than likely based on Seaton's recommendation. (For further information about Holman Fred Stephens see *The Col. Stephens Railways in Kent* by Peter A.Harding).

The contract to build the line, which featured several very deep cuttings and two short tunnels, was awarded to Mr.J.T.Firbank. He was also involved with the Metropolitan Railway at that time as contractor for their line between Aylesbury and Quainton Road. For the Cranbrook & Paddock Wood Railway contract, Firbank was represented on-site by Mr.George Throssel and used a 0-6-0 saddle tank built by Fox Walker, appropriately named 'Fox', and another 0-6-0 saddle tank built by Manning Wardle called 'Wrexham'.

Construction began from Paddock Wood to Horsmonden in the spring of 1890, while powers were later obtained in 1892 to divert the Hawkhurst extension to a less severely graded route. This would now place the terminus at Gills Green, well over a mile north of Hawkhurst. At about this time, there was also a suggestion to continue the line from Hawkhurst and link up with the Lydd Railway Company at Appledore, thus connecting the Weald with Dungeness and New Romney. Despite the chairman of the Lydd Railway Company being Alfred Mellor Watkin who, (as we have already noted) was also a director of the Cranbrook & Paddock Wood Railway, the idea came to nothing.

The station buildings were single storey corrugated iron constructions and were built by Mancktelow Bros. of Horsmonden. They were also responsible for building at each station a fine three storey brick stationmaster's house, two of which (at Goudhurst and Cranbrook) were built on the platforms adjoining the station buildings.

The signals were erected by Messrs McKenzie & Holland and the line was worked by Tyers No.6 tablet with each station being equipped with the relevant instruments.

Although many reports (including the first edition of this publication) state that the line was officially opened on October 1st 1892 from Paddock Wood Junction to

Hope Mill Station (for Goudhurst and Lamberhurst), it actually opened on Monday September 12th 1892, after Major Francis Marindin (of the Board of Trade) had carried out an inspection of the line using two engines to test the strength of the bridges on September 3rd 1892. The inspection proved to be satisfactory and the Friday September 9th 1892 edition of the *Kent & Sussex Courier* carried the following announcement:-

---

SOUTH EASTERN RAILWAY.

OPENING OF
CRANBROOK & PADDOCK
WOOD LINE.

THE above Line will be OPENED for Passenger and Goods Traffic on

MONDAY, SEPTEMBER 12th,

TO

HORSMONDEN AND HOPE MILL

(For GOUDHURST & LAMBERHURST).

MYLES FENTON,
General Manager.

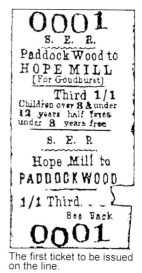

The first ticket to be issued on the line.

The Saturday September 17th 1892 edition of the *Kent Messenger* reported the grand opening of the first section of the Cranbrook & Paddock Wood Railway as follows:-

The opening of this line as far as Hope Mill Station, Goudhurst, took place on Monday last, and was attended with considerable excitement both in Goudhurst and Horsmonden. The first train left Hope Mill at 8.25 a.m., and as all passengers were allowed to ride to Paddock Wood Junction and back during the day free, all trains were well patronised, not a few finding themselves the occupants of a railway carriage for the first time in their lives. The engine, which was draped in front with the Union Jack, while the body of the locomotive was festooned with hops, and very hearty was the cheering which greeted its progress all along the line. In the evening at the Gun Inn, Horsmonden, a large party dined in celebration of the long looked for event. Several loads of hops and fruit were despatched during the day.

To celebrate the opening day, the farmhouse and oast houses at Hope Mill, which were owned by Mr. Edward Clemetson, were decorated with bunting and some of the streets in Horsmonden were also decorated.

The ceremonial first train was drawn by a Cudworth E1 class 2-4-0 No.112 which arrived at Hope Mill Station with five very quaint old four wheel carriages and two brake vans. The driver was Mr. Frank Martin and the fireman was Mr. G.F.Cheal. The guard was Mr. William Hollingworth, whilst travelling inspectors Philpott and Osborne also accompanied the train. The E1 class was originally introduced by James I'Anson Cudworth (the SER locomotive superintendent from 1845 to 1876) as the "118" class in 1863. When James Stirling became the SER locomotive superintendent in 1878, he introduced a simple lettered classification. The "118" became the E class. When Stirling had any of these locomotives reboilered, they became E1's.

The appointed stationmaster at Hope Mill was a Mr. Field, who it was understood had been transferred from Reading.

The ceremonial first train at Hope Mill Station (later re-named Goudhurst) on Monday September 12th 1892. Resident engineer Holman Fred Stephens is the tall man with light trousers, standing next to the locomotive.   Col. Stephens Railway Museum, Tenterden

Resident engineer Holman Fred Stephens (left) with the local Squire and Vicar at Hope Mill Station on the same day. The Vicar is thought to be the Rev. H. H. Wilford (Curate at Horsmonden) who was thanked during the celebration dinner at the Gun Inn, Horsmonden for 'coming amongst them as one of themselves'.   National Railway Museum, York

7

Another view of the ceremonial first train at Hope Mill Station on Monday September 12th 1892.

The newly opened station at Hope Mill.

The Friday October 21st 1892 edition of the *Kent & Sussex Courier* reported the following interesting item:-

The new station "Hope Mill" was opened as a postal telegraph office on Wednesday and the first message was sent by Mr.E.Beech of the Chequers Inn, Lamberhurst, to Mr.W.Gurr of the same place.

Apart from the confusion of the opening date of the line, there also seems to be some confusion as to the exact date of the re-naming of Hope Mill Station. The following note which throws some light on the subject appeared in the *Kent & Sussex Courier* on Friday November 25th 1892:-

GOUDHURST

THE RAILWAY - We understand that the amount of traffic, both passenger and goods, on this new line has somewhat surprised everybody, so much so that additional siding accommodation will have to be provided to prevent blocking of traffic in subsequent years. Our village station was named Hope Mill after the name of the part of the parish in which it was erected. A petition was presented to the Railway Company, and henceforth our station will be known by the name of "Goudhurst".

While the line between Goudhurst and Hawkhurst was being built, a 'substantial tea', which was organised by Hawkhurst residents who had made '188 good meat pies' was served to 160 navvies in Mrs. Eaton's barn at Badgers Oak Farm (near where the Badgers Oak Tunnel was being built) on April 20th 1892. The speakers were Rev.A.Harrison, Mr.E.Hardcastle and Mr.Henry Maynard.

A very sad event was reported in the March 23rd 1893 edition of the *Maidstone Journal* when a workman on the line was buried alive at Badgers Oak after tons of earth fell on him.

J.T.Firbank's men constructing the line near Badgers Oak Tunnel in 1892. The general good conduct of the navvies (who were described at the celebrations of the opening of the first section of the line as a hearty and jolly lot of fellows) was met with much praise.   Author's Collection

Cranbrook Station being completed, with the contractors 0-6-0 saddle tank "Fox" in the distance and the navvies and their temporary track in the foreground.   Author's Collection

The extension from Goudhurst to Hawkhurst was opened to all traffic on Monday September 4th 1893. The *Kent & Sussex Courier* reported this event in their Friday September 8th edition, as follows:-

PADDOCK WOOD AND HAWKHURST RAILWAY

The opening of the second section of this line was celebrated by a public dinner at the Queen's Hotel, Hawkhurst, on Monday evening, when about 60 sat down to a capital repast under the presidency of Lord Medway, supported by Mr.F.Heath (Vice-Chairman), Col.Ready, Mr.E.Hardcastle, Mr.A.Hardcastle, Mr.H.Nevill, Mr.W.F.Winch, Mr.T.Hall, Mr.J.M.Durrant, and a representative company.

After the usual loyal toasts had been duly honoured, the Chairman next gave "Success to the new line", coupled with the names of Messrs. Seaton and Stephens, and referred to the important bearing on the prosperity of the neighbourhood that the opening up of railway facilities must have and the great satisfaction felt that this long talked of line was at last an accomplished fact.

The healths of "The Chairman", "The Vice-Chairman", "The Visitors", and "The Press" concluded the toast list, which was enlivened by some capital harmony, Mr.Whitburn being the principal vocalist.

The ceremonial first train at Cranbrook Station after the second section of the line was opened between Goudhurst and Hawkhurst on September 4th 1893.   Col. Stephens Railway Museum, Tenterden

10

It seems strange that the SER was prepared to have some of their limited financial strength taken up by supporting such places like Cranbrook and Hawkhurst, but the SER Chairman Sir Edward Watkin stated at their General Meeting on January 25th 1894, that they could not have gone to Parliament for further powers if the obligation to serve Cranbrook had not been fulfilled. It is ironic that Cranbrook, whose name took pride of place in the title of the local company promoted to build the line, was in fact nearly two miles away from the village of Hartley, where the station was built. While reporting about the preliminary trials of the bridges and permanent way of the second section of the Cranbrook & Paddock Wood Railway prior to the inspection of the Board of Trade, the Saturday September 2nd 1893 edition of the *Kent Messenger* included the following interesting paragraph:-

We hear on good authority that a number of influential home dwellers are prepared to guarantee to the SER the cost of constructing a light line from Hartley station into Cranbrook town, the approximate expense of which, independent of plant etc., and provided the land be acquired on fair and equitable terms, is put at £10,000. The distance is nearly two miles.

The very wording "light line" could have referred to a type of tramway but this line was never built and was probably more an afterthought from some of the influential people of Cranbrook. They were regretful of the fact that the original plan for the Cranbrook & Paddock Wood Railway to actually reach the town had been changed when some landowners had asked too much for their land and the line was re-routed from Hartley and extended towards Hawkhurst.

Cranbrook Station in the early 1920's.   Lens of Sutton

The approach to Hawkhurst Station at a similar time.   Lens of Sutton

With the line from Paddock Wood to Hawkhurst completed and up and running, the Cranbrook & Paddock Wood Railway Company ceased to exist on January 29th 1900 when it was absorbed by the SER. Some 18 months earlier, the SER had ended their rivalry with the LCDR by negotiating an arrangement whereby both companies remained separate but worked together under the heading of the South Eastern & Chatham Railway Management Committee (SE&CR). From this time onwards, the line seems to have always been referred to as the Hawkhurst branch.

An early view of Goudhurst Station, showing a train arriving at the down platform. The small waiting shelter (on the right of the photograph) was later removed. Author's Collection

Horsmonden Station, soon after the line had opened. Lens of Sutton

Tenterden was not of course involved in this line and in fact, had to wait until 1900 when the Rother Valley Railway (with Holman Fred Stephens as engineer) was opened from Robertsbridge on the Tonbridge-Hastings main line as far as Rolvenden Station, then named Tenterden. The short extension to Tenterden Town came into being in April 1903.

In the same year a further Light Railway Order was obtained for an extension from Tenterden Town to Headcorn on the Tonbridge-Ashford main line and in the following year the company name was changed to the Kent & East Sussex Railway. In 1900 the Rother Valley Railway had acquired powers in the name of the Cranbrook & Tenterden Railway Company for a line to link these two small towns and the authorisation was even renewed in 1904. This line was never built, but still continued to figure in the Kent & East Sussex Railway Company's reports until 1937.

Although the Sunday service on the Hawkhurst branch ceased on January 1st 1917, and was never reinstated, the line continued its tranquil existence in the hands of the SE&CR until the 1923 grouping which saw it become part of the newly formed Southern Railway. From this time onwards things stayed very much the same and even in 1948, when the Southern Railway passed into the hands of the British Railways Southern Region after nationalisation, the line seemed untouched by any possible change.

C class 0-6-0 No.1225 embedded in an embankment just outside Goudhurst Station after crashing through some siding buffers. Fortunately, nobody was hurt. February 18th 1948.
Gordon Batchelor

On July 6th 1950, Her Majesty Queen Elizabeth (later of course the Queen Mother) visited the National Sanatorium at Benenden and travelled on the branch to Cranbrook Station and then by car the rest of the way. The "Royal Train" was pulled by a Maunsell E1 class 4-4-0 No.31067 and the special pullman carriage used by Her Majesty was called 'Malaga'. The author remembers the occasion well as at that time he was a six year old schoolboy at Goudhurst and the whole village school marched down to the station waving Union Jacks to witness this special event. Her Majesty duly waved to the crowd as the train slowly passed through the station.

Over the next few years, fears for the future of the line grew and by the early 1960's when hop-picking traffic ceased, it came as little surprise when it was announced that the line would close.

The branch officially closed on Saturday June 10th 1961, although the following day, a special train organised by the Locomotive Club of Great Britain and called "The South Eastern Limited", went down the branch to Hawkhurst and back. Later that day, the same train travelled over the remaining portion of the Kent & East Sussex Railway from Robertsbridge to Tenterden (the section from Headcorn to Tenterden having closed in 1954).

Description of the Route

Like many similar rural branch lines, the Hawkhurst line suffered from the inconvenient placing of its stations. Horsmonden was the only station on the branch which was located close to its village. Goudhurst was a mile away and some 250 ft higher than its station. Cranbrook is nearly two miles away from the small village of Hartley where its station was. Hawkhurst is about 1¼ miles from Gills Green where its station and the line's terminus was.

Paddock Wood has always been a typical SER station and received its name from a small wood which was cut down for its construction. The station only acquired its present name in 1844, having been known as Maidstone Road until then. In those days there was not even a farmhouse in the vicinity, which makes the station the oldest building in the small town that has grown up since the coming of the railway.

The station layout includes two through platforms which are served by loops off the main lines so that fast trains can overtake stopping trains. At the eastern end of each platform a short bay was provided, the 270 ft long one on the down side being used for Maidstone trains and the 194 ft long one on the up side being the Hawkhurst branch bay. All the branch trains started here although for many years the last up train ran through to Tonbridge mainly because of the through vans it hauled and also because the engine was serviced at the Tonbridge shed.

Swatlands Siding
Christie & Vesley's Siding
Granary Sidings
Keylands Sidings
Goods Shed
Carriage Road
Station Building
Hernden Siding
Long Siding
←To Tonbridge
Top Yard
Station Building
Dock Siding
Signal Box
Hawkhurst Branch Bay
Hay Siding
Old Muck Siding
New Muck Siding
To Marden ►
To Hawkhurst→
To Maidstone
Slip Road

PADDOCK WOOD

H class 0-4-4T No.31523 waits with the train for Hawkhurst in the branch bay at Paddock Wood Station . July 23rd 1957. Alan A. Jackson

The signal box at Paddock Wood Station in 1961, with the single track of the Hawkhurst branch below. J.J.Smith

The single track of the Hawkhurst branch passed under the signal box (which was built high up on girders) and ran parallel to the main line for nearly three quarters of a mile before gradually diverging. On some occasions the Hawkhurst and main line trains started simultaneously and there is no doubt that many times a good healthy race was enjoyed both by crews and passengers alike. The branch gradually turned away to the south and ran on the level, passing under a road bridge and through some intensely farmed country.

The Hawkhurst branch (on the right) diverging to the south from the main line.　　B.R.Hart

The line then passed over Willow Lane level crossing and skirted a series of orchards and hop gardens before climbing a gradient of 1 in 78 until it came to Churn Lane Siding, which was on a 1 in 66. Here there was a level crossing, and a siding which was unused for public traffic from 1940. In later years, it was used to store wagons awaiting repair or the scrapyard at Ashford.

←To Paddock Wood　　Level Crossing　　**CHURN LANE SIDING**　　To Horsmonden →　　Tompsett's Brick Siding

Not far from Churn Lane was an accommodation crossing on a drive to a large farm. In 1938 the branch freight would stop here for hop pockets (sacks) to be loaded into a box wagon.

After passing under another road bridge, the gradients now quickly climbed from 1 in 78 to 1 in 66 and speed soon dropped. Though the branch traffic was used to this and carried on along its journey, some of the heavier "hop-pickers" specials would sometimes slip and come to grief.

The line then ran on the level through a valley known as Swigs Hole on an embankment which averaged about 42 ft in height and about half a mile in length. It crossed a small lane to a farm by a bridge before reaching a deep, wooded cutting which was followed by a short 86 yard tunnel, and continued in a deeper cutting before passing under a small bridge carrying a country lane. It then reached picturesque Horsmonden Station, 4³/₈ miles from Paddock Wood.

The 86 yard long Horsmonden Tunnel.　　D.Cullum

Horsmonden only had a single 300 ft long platform on the up side plus a loop, which looked like a passing loop but was in fact used to serve an adjoining fruit packing warehouse, where loaded wagons of (mainly) apples were despatched to all parts of the country. The station building was a single storey corrugated iron construction with a short wooded platform awning - the type of building which became synonymous with lines Holman Fred Stephens was involved with. At the back of the station lay the goods yard and the stationmaster's house, which was a three-storey building with dormer windows and faced the road rather than the railway. The village, with its houses fringing a broad green, lies a short distance to the west of the former station.

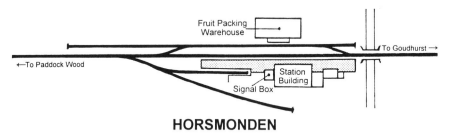

HORSMONDEN

Horsmonden Station, looking towards Goudhurst. Lens of Sutton

Beyond Horsmonden, the line crossed the road by a plate girder bridge adjoining the station and ran on the level before crossing a small country lane by a similar bridge. It then ran along the Teise Valley toward the Wealden hills. It passed over Smallbridge level crossing, and with gradients falling at 1 in 117, 110 and 213, passed through hop gardens, crossing over the River Teise before reaching Goudhurst Station (which was just over 6 miles from Paddock Wood).

Goudhurst had a fully signalled passing loop and two platforms - the only station on the line that had. In later years the first up and down passenger trains of the day crossed here. The up platform, which was 293 ft long, not only had the usual corrugated iron station building but also the three-storey brick built stationmaster's house with prominent dormer windows adjoining it, giving quite a bold impression for a small country branch station. In earlier years the 301 ft long down platform also had a small covered shelter but this was later dismantled. Any passing motorist driving over the level crossing to the south side of the station could easily have thought it was a main line or at least a secondary line, the single track and passing loop curved together as far as the eye could see in both directions.

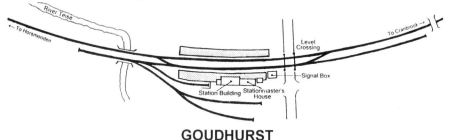

GOUDHURST

A fine view of Goudhurst Station, looking towards Cranbrook.   Lens of Sutton

The pleasant village of Goudhurst stands on the edge of one of the highest ridges of the Weald and is a mile away from the site of the station. The views from the church tower are most picturesque. In every direction one sees the characteristic groups of oast houses with white cowls slowly turning in the breeze and standing like sentries on guard over the farm buildings, so much a part of the Wealden scenery. The fact that the village is a mile away and some 250 ft higher than the station must have been very disheartening to any unsuspecting heavily-laden passenger who arrived without prior knowledge, especially as there was no connecting bus route.

The line now followed a tributary of the Teise passing under a series of three road bridges, while slowly circling Goudhurst village, for about a mile until it came to Pattenden Siding. Here the odd wagon load of "shoddy" (woollen waste) was left which would fertilize the hops. Nearby Smugley Farm obtained its name from local smuggling days, being within easy reach of the Romney Marsh where illicit cargoes were run.

To Cranbrook →

←To Goudhurst

PATTENDEN SIDING

From Pattenden Siding the climb was now on again, with a 1 in 60, 85 and 260 up the narrow valley through woodlands. The scenery here is some of the most attractive in the Weald and the locomotives would blast their way up the hillside past Forge Farm then on under a small bridge carrying a track, before passing Furnace Farm. It then reached Cranbrook Station, just 10 miles from Paddock Wood. As explained earlier, Cranbrook Station was at the small village of Hartley, some two miles from Cranbrook itself. The station, like Horsmonden, only had one 300 ft long platform on the down side and a 'goods only' loop. It was like Goudhurst in as much as it had the usual corrugated iron station building and the stationmaster's house on the platform. The spacious goods yard lay on the same side as the platform, as did the large red-brick goods shed. A warehouse, which was used by a corn merchant was at the Goudhurst end of the goods yard.

Goods Shed

Warehouse

Station Building

Stationmaster's House

Signal Box

To Hawkhurst →

←To Goudhurst

CRANBROOK

Cranbrook Station, looking towards Hawkhurst. September 22nd 1951.   R.F.Roberts

18

The small town of Cranbrook, with its spacious church and several fine old buildings, recalls its former importance as a centre of the cloth weaving industry established by Flemish immigrants in the fourteenth century. The windmill on the outskirts of the town was erected in 1814, and is said to be one of the largest in England.

From Cranbrook the line passed under a small bridge which lead to a farm, and then climbed a 1 in 80 for about half a mile until it reached the summit. A short distance beyond the summit the line passed through the charmingly named Badgers Oak Tunnel, 178 yards long. Beyond the tunnel the line dropped down a 1 in 80 until it reached the terminus at Hawkhurst, on the level.

Badgers Oak Tunnel, looking towards Cranbrook.   Pamlin Prints

The approach to the station was along an embankment and over two plate girder bridges which crossed two small country lanes. The siding entrance was situated just over the second bridge and extended into an adjoining wood yard (later to take over the whole station area). The station stood in an isolated, elevated position at Gills Green, which was 11¹/₂ miles from Paddock Wood, and was laid out as a through station in case the line was extended for any of the earlier proposals. On arrival, passengers were treated to fine views over the Weald towards the Romney Marsh.

The layout consisted of a single 308 ft long platform on the down side with the corrugated iron station building, similar to that at Horsmonden plus a short 140 ft long bay platform. A run-round loop extended almost as far as the outer siding point with a short neck which, although not necessary for the usual traffic of the 0-4-4T's and pull-and-push units, did allow a 4-4-0 to run round a six carriage train. About half way along the loop was a signal box and a water tower. Beyond the water tower the line to the engine shed ran off into two lanes but one of these was lifted when the shed closed in 1931. After the engine shed closed, all the lines motive power was supplied by the Tonbridge shed. Behind the short platform bay lay the loading dock and the very large goods shed. The stationmaster's house was situated to the south of the elevated position of the station and was approached from the road.

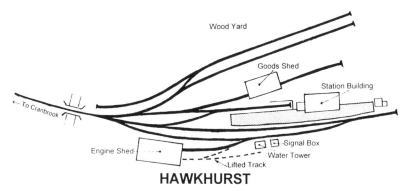

HAWKHURST

As previously mentioned, the station was about 1¼ miles from Hawkhurst, a small town on the main road from London to Rye. The author remembers from his childhood the covered footpath of the main street (the colonnade) as being reminiscent of a wild west cowboy town. Keeping to that tradition, the town was once the headquarters of the Hawkhurst Gang, a powerful group of smugglers who terrorised the Kent and Sussex coasts.

Hawkhurst Station, looking towards the buffer stops. August 3rd 1946.   R.F.Roberts

Gradient Profile

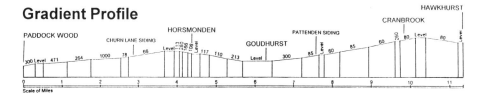

Motive Power and Rolling Stock

When people remember the motive power and rolling stock on the Hawkhurst branch, they probably think of a two carriage pull-and-push set drawn by a Wainwright H class 0-4-4T, which was the usual branch working at the time of closure. The H class had taken over from the former LCDR Kirtley R and R1 class 0-4-4T's, which were withdrawn in the mid-1950's. The pull-and-push trains were worked by a special regulation without guards, provided there were no vans to pick up or detach. The H class was "constructed", not "built", at Ashford during the Wainwright era and used extensively for branch line and suburban passenger duties. Unfortunately, only one locomotive of this class has survived. The engine is No. 31263 and can now be seen at the Bluebell Railway in Sussex. No. 31263 worked both the Hawkhurst and Westerham branches during its days at the Tonbridge shed.

As mentioned in the history of the line, the first locomotive was a Cudworth E1 class 2-4-0 (formerly the 118 class) and this class, and the former Ramsbottom "Ironclad" class 2-4-0's (which became the L class under James Stirling), worked the passenger service for the first few years, but by the early 1900's were superceded by Stirling Q class 0-4-4T's. Occasionally Stirling A, B and F class 4-4-0's were seen but these were mainly for the hop-picking specials.

After the 1914-18 war, the SE&CR decided to bring their local service up to scratch. To do this, six former LCDR Kirtley R class 0-4-4T's were fitted with pull-and-push fittings. The motor train system applied to the R class was very successful and used the Westinghouse air pump, replacing the earlier wire and pulley arrangement. This class worked the line from the post-war period onwards, but by the 1930's the R class was joined at Tonbridge by the R1 class. The R and R1's mainly worked the branch until the mid-1950's, when they were finally withdrawn from Tonbridge and replaced by the Wainwright H class, although Stirling O1 class 0-6-0's were sometimes used for passenger trains in the 1940's.

H class 0-4-4T No.31543 with a pull-and-push set at Cranbrook Station. October 15th 1960.
H.B.Priestley

B class 4-4-0 No.A458 at Hawkhurst Station. July 17th 1926. The late H.C.Casserley

The early goods trains were pulled by a Stirling O class 0-6-0, but in 1915 the Tonbridge shed managed to obtain the services of a shunter from the Folkestone quay, a Manning Wardle 0-6-0 saddle tank. This engine proved unsuitable for shunting in the local goods yard and occasionally found itself pulling the lighter Hawkhurst goods trains instead. With the increase of heavy goods traffic brought about by the First World War, Tonbridge received its share of Wainwright C class 0-6-0's so the Manning Wardle tank returned to the Folkestone quay.

Goods traffic, comprising mainly of fruit, hops, grain and timber being sent out, while coal, fertilizers and feeding stuffs were brought in, proved of some importance after the First World War. But after the Second World War it declined following the increase in mechanized road transport. Hops were conveyed by road to Paddock Wood, while fruit went by road direct to London. In the late 1950's the Paddock Wood diesel shunter was used for goods trains, but that duty later reverted to the C class 0-6-0's. Other engines which were used on goods traffic in the later years were former LBSCR C2X class 0-6-0's and E4 class 0-6-2's.

A stranger to the line in the shape of former LBSCR Stroudley D1 class 0-4-2T No.2234, leaving Cranbrook with the branch train for Hawkhurst. July 22nd 1933. The late H.C.Casserley

During the hop-picking season the specials and the weekend hop-pickers "friends" excursions would run direct to the branch from London Bridge Low Level, and called at New Cross or New Cross Gate on the way. They were usually pulled by D class or E class 4-4-0's or the rebuilt D1 and E1 classes.

Other special traffic was for the boarding schools in the area. Benenden Girls School would have a special to and from Charing Cross, which was made up of six corridor carriages and pulled by either a E1 or D1 class 4-4-0. Although Cranbrook was the station for Benenden, the special would continue to Hawkhurst to enable the engine to run round. Cranbrook Boys School would have to make do with the service trains which were increased to four carriages. In the later years of the branch, pot plants from local nurseries for F.W.Woolworths branches across the country were railed from Hawkhurst. Every day, up to four 4-wheel utility vans were loaded behind the 8.06 p.m. locomotive from Hawkhurst, which ran through to Tonbridge for the vans to be transferred. About one million pot plants a year were railed and this traffic was rumoured to have brought in an annual income of about £50,000. This is probably one of the reasons why the branch lasted as long as it did.

One brief but interesting visitor to the line was the Sentinel-Cammell steam railbus No.6, which was built in 1933 for the Southern Railway to the requirements of Mr.R.E.L.Maunsell, for service on the Brighton to Devils Dyke branch. By early 1936 the number of passengers was more than it could handle, and the railbus was transferred in March of that year to Tonbridge to work the Westerham branch, where it was unpopular with passengers and drivers. In October 1936 it was tried out on the Hawkhurst branch and lasted a month before moving on to work the evening services between Tonbridge and Edenbridge, until April 1937. After laying idle behind the Tonbridge shed it was scrapped at Ashford works in 1946.

Carriage stock ranged from the ancient SER 4-wheelers which worked the first train and lasted on the line for at least twenty years, to the former LCDR three carriage 6-wheel sets. Pull-and-push sets were made up of the converted former SE&CR steam railcars, former LBSCR and London & South Western Railway (LSWR) sets, and various hybrid sets, until the final days of the line when converted Maunsell stock was used.

R class 0-4-4T No.31675 with a branch train at Cranbrook Station. September 22nd 1951.
R.F.Roberts

C class 0-6-0 No.31271 at Cranbrook Station. September 22nd 1951.   R.F.Roberts

The driver takes up his position in pull-and-push unit No.739 at Hawkhurst Station while the fireman remains with R1 class 0-4-4T No.31700 at the far end. May 21st 1949.John H. Meredith

E4 class 0-6-2T No.32580 at Cranbrook Station with a surprisingly short 'hop-pickers' special. September 22nd 1951.   R.F.Roberts

'Hop-pickers' Specials

During hop-picking, the Hawkhurst branch took a large amount of extra traffic. The number of specials varied from year to year - in 1912 there were 26 specials required, with as many as 350 people arriving on each train. This caused all sorts of problems for the local traffic.

In later years the hop-pickers specials were more organised and did not interfere with the normal service trains. A "Hop Control Centre" was set up at Paddock Wood to co-ordinate the special traffic. This worked so well that "hoppers" could catch their train at London Bridge and be taken straight to the nearest station to the farm at which they were to stay and work. Sometimes the farmers even met them.

The number of specials intensified at weekends when it was common for the hop-pickers friends and relations to visit them. On return, there were sometimes as many as eleven trains to London Bridge from the hop fields, all arriving within the space of four hours. Of these, three would travel up the main line via Sevenoaks, two from the Hawkhurst branch, four from the Maidstone line and one from Bodiam.

The bulk of the specials ran on Sundays when the Hawkhurst branch was normally closed. Hawkhurst Station would receive up to six trains a day. Fresh locomotives would be sent down in the evenings from Tonbridge. By 1959 the hop-pickers traffic had dropped to only one two-carriage train on a Sunday with a return through working to London Bridge. The normal weekday service was considered adequate for all other needs.

As mentioned in the description of the route, the climb from Churn Lane towards Horsmonden was 1 in 66 and often gave the hop-pickers specials a certain amount of bother. One such occasion was on September 29th 1951, when the "Hop-pickers Return Special" was being worked up, tender first, from Paddock Wood. The engine was D class 4-4-0 No.31729 and it slipped to a standstill just short of Horsmonden Tunnel. When working in reverse, the D class sanding gear could not be used, so a re-start was impossible. The fireman walked on through the tunnel to Horsmonden Station where he telephoned for assistance. Help arrived in the shape of C class 0-6-0 No.31717, which assisted at the rear until Horsmonden was reached. There it ran round and piloted for the rest of the journey.

Hop-pickers await the arrival of their 'Hop-pickers Return Special' at Goudhurst Station on September 29th 1951. This special train ran from Hawkhurst to London Bridge and was double headed by C class 0-6-0 No.31717 and D class 4-4-0 No.31729.   K.G.Carr

Timetables and Tickets

1892
(When the line opened)

UP	Week Days				Sundays		
	A.M.	P.M.	P.M.	P.M.	A.M.	A.M	P.M.	P.M.
Hope Mill	8.25	12.10	1.32	5.30	8.35	9.30	7.30	8.25
Horsmonden	8.58	12.16	1.38	5.36	8.41	9.36	7.35	8.31
Paddock Wood	9. 8	12.26	1.48	5.46	8.51	9.46	7.46	8.41

DOWN	Week Days					Sundays		
	A.M.	P.M.	P.M.	P.M.	P.M.	A.M.	A.M	P.M.	P.M.
Paddock Wood	9.42	12.35	2. 8	4.48	6.35	7.43	9. 5	7. 6	8. 3
Horsmonden	9.52	12.45	2.18	4.58	6.45	7.53	9.15	7.16	8.13
Hope Mill	9.58	12.51	2.24	5. 4	6.51	7.59	9.21	7.22	8.19

Sunday service ceased on January 1st 1917, and was never reinstated.

1921

DOWN	Week Days Only					
	A.M.	A.M.	P.M.	P.M.	P.M.	P.M.
Paddock Wood	8.30	11. 8	1.50	4.30	5.58	7.32
Horsmonden	8.39	11.17	1.59	4.39	6. 7	7.41
Goudhurst	8.43	11.21	2. 3	4.43	6.12	7.46
Cranbrook	8.52	11.30	2.12	4.52	6.25	7.55
Hawkhurst	8.57	11.35	2.17	4.57	6.30	8. 0

UP	Week Days Only					
	A.M.	A.M.	P.M.	P.M.	P.M.	P.M.
Hawkhurst	7.49	9. 5	11.44	3.39	4.57	6. 1	6.44
Cranbrook	7.54	9.10	11.49	3.44	5. 2	6. 6	6.49
Goudhurst	8. 1	9.17	11.58	3.51	5. 9	6.13	6.56
Horsmonden	8. 6	9.22	12. 4	3.56	5.14	6.20	7. 1
Paddock Wood	8.16	9.32	12.14	4. 6	5.24	6.30	7.11

Summer 1952

DOWN	Week Days Only							
	A.M.	A.M.	P.M.	P.M. S.O.	P.M.	P.M.	P.M.
Paddock Wood	7.35	9. 7	12.24	2.24	4.25	5.50	7.28
Horsmonden	7.45	9.17	12.34	2.32	4.35	6. 0	7.38
Goudhurst	7.54	9.23	12.40	2.40	4.41	6. 6	7.44
Cranbrook	8. 5	9.32	12.49	2.49	4.50	6.15	7.53
Hawkhurst	8.10	9.37	12.54	2.54	4.55	6.20	7.58

UP	Week Days Only							
	A.M.	A.M.	A.M.	P.M.	P.M. S.O.	P.M.	P.M.	P.M.
Hawkhurst	7.40	8.24	9.43	12.58	3.12	5. 5	6.35	8. 7
Cranbrook	7.44	8.28	9.47	1. 2	3.16	5. 9	6.39	8.11
Goudhurst	7.53	8.37	9.56	1.11	3.25	5.18	6.48	8.20
Horsmonden	7.59	8.43	10. 2	1.17	3.31	5.24	6.54	8.26
Paddock Wood	8.10	8.54	10.13	1.28	3.42	5.35	7. 5	8.37

SO   Saturdays Only

Tickets from the G.R.Croughton Collection.

Closure

Towards the end of the 1950's, for many reasons the line's future appeared to be in some doubt. After being part of a way of life for several generations, the hop-picking traffic rapidly dwindled and by the early 1960's had ceased as far as the railways in the South East were concerned. This was due partly to the introduction of mechanized harvesting but with a working holiday becoming a thing of the past, this would probably have happened in any case.

Apart from the daily average number of passengers, which never seemed to top 200, a large number of school children were carried. But even this was lost when the local Education Authority contracted with the Maidstone & District Motor Company to transport the children by bus.

Connections to and from London were poor and anyone who wanted to reach Tunbridge Wells, from Horsmonden, Goudhurst or Cranbrook would prefer to go direct by bus (the famous Maidstone & District No.97) from the village centre rather than change twice on the railway. A bus service was also now running from Goudhurst to Maidstone so this cut out any passengers in that direction.

Goods traffic had fallen away (as previously mentioned) so it came as no surprise when talk of the line's closure spread. It was rumoured locally that the line would become electified, but this was only a pipe dream and the dreaded closure notice appeared at all stations on the branch.

The last day's public service to Hawkhurst was on Saturday June 10th 1961. A pair of C class 0-6-0's replaced the usual H class tanks for this special day and even the B.B.C. had a television cameraman at Paddock Wood to record the 9.07 a.m. leaving the junction station. The Tonbridge crew joined in the day's proceedings by optimistically chalking on the locomotive's cabside the following:- *"Shed no tears for the single track, for perhaps we may come back. And if we do, you can be sure, we'll see you all again once more"*.

Halfway through the day, former LSWR pull-and-push set No.656 and a further Maunsell corridor carriage were added to the train, which was now being pulled by C class No.31588. Every seat seemed to be occupied by railway enthusiasts, photographers and local people making a last sentimental journey.

CLOSURE OF HAWKHURST BRANCH RAILWAY LINE

On and from MONDAY, 12th JUNE 1961, all services will be withdrawn from the Hawkhurst branch line and HORSMONDEN, GOUDHURST, CRANBROOK and HAWKHURST stations, also Churn Lane and Pattenden sidings, closed.

British Railways will continue to provide collection and delivery services for parcels and freight sundries throughout the area and facilities for truck load traffic exist at other stations in the vicinity.

Further information may be obtained from the Station Master at PADDOCK WOOD (Telephone: 322) or TONBRIDGE (Telephone: 2266) or from the Line Traffic Manager, Southern Region, British Railways, South Eastern Division, 61 Queen Street, London, E.C.4. (Telephone: WATerloo 5151, Ext. 227).

Enquiries in regard to bus services in the area should be addressed to:-
The Maidstone & District Motor Services Ltd.
Knightrider House, Maidstone - Telephone: 2211
St. John's Road, Tunbridge Wells - 2022t
Opera House Buildings, Tunbridge Wells - 1700
Sandhurst Road, Hawkhurst - 3168

Closure notice at Goudhurst Station. June 3rd 1961.

C class 0-6-0 No.31588 with the branch train at Cranbrook Station on Saturday June 10th 1961, the last day of public service.   A.E.Bennett

The Friday June 16th 1961 edition of the *Kent & Sussex Courier* describes the final train from Paddock Wood in the following way:-

Parasols and boaters recall bygone days

Crowds cheered on Paddock Wood Station on Saturday. But they did not cheer a triumph; rather they gave the acclaim a British crowd will always have for a gallant loser.

There was a forced note about the gaiety of the bunting lining the coaches. Fog detonators cracked under the wheels as the train, whistle screaming, pulled out of Paddock Wood for the last time.

"It is a very sad affair amid all the jollification. For 70 years men in the fields have known the time from the trains", said Goudhurst Parish Council chairman, Cdr.C.E.Millson, who travelled on the train.

Cdr. Millson and Mr.S.G.Calcutt, chairman of Cranbrook Parish Council, travelled in Victorian costume in a party organised by Vicki Millson, Nicholas Thornely and Richard Coleman.

"Parish councils and the rural council are watching the interests of local people - especially traders - now the line is gone", said Cdr. Millson.

Wreaths on engine

The first three tickets issued on the line are still in existence. The first taken out by his father, belongs to Sir George Jessel. Tony Coleman has the second (his grandfather's), and the third, now with Vicki Millson, has also come down through two generations.

Paddock Wood stationmaster, Mr.E.G.Coffin, was suitably dressed as an undertaker, and the engine, driven by Mr.A.J.Mitchell, was wreathed like a bier.

Mr.A.E.Hardinge, a locomotive inspector from London Bridge, accompanied fireman R.Haines on the footplate. Guard Frank Ransom was in charge.

Large crowds, many people with cameras, packed each station on what used to be before picking machines became popular, the "hoppers line".

Posters on the coaches read: "Last train, 1892-1961 : R.I.P." Many railwaymen, off-duty, came along for the ride. One said: "It's a shame - and not just because it means fewer jobs".

From the footplate of the engine at Hawkhurst, Miss Ann Payne, daughter of well known bandleader Jack Payne, raised her glass to toast the last train to leave the terminus on its journey back to Paddock Wood.

And so, by the end of the day, the Hawkhurst branch line was finished. No more would its pull-and-push trains puff and blow their way through some of the most delightful countryside anyone could wish to see.

On the following day the Locomotive Club of Great Britain organised a "Farewell to Steam" tour in the South East, and went down the Hawkhurst branch and also the remaining portion of the Kent & East Sussex Railway from Robertsbridge to Tenterden. This special train was called "The South Eastern Limited" and was lengthened from seven to nine carriages due to the high demand for tickets. To work the special train over the Hawkhurst branch, O1 class 0-6-0 No.31065, and C class 0-6-0 No.31592 were used. This train proved to be the last public train to run to and from Hawkhurst.

The Locomotive Club of Great Britain special train "The South Eastern Limited" approaching Horsmonden on the return run from Hawkhurst. June 11th 1961.   S.C.Nash

The Present Scene

Since June 1961, nature has quickly reclaimed much of the right-of-way of the Hawkhurst branch. In 1964 the track was lifted by the Demolition and Construction Company. Some embankments have been bulldozed, and some cuttings have been filled in and levelled. Certain parts of the line have been taken into orchards and fields.

Track lifting at Goudhurst Station. April 25th 1964.   R.C.Riley

A look at the whole route shows that Paddock Wood Station on the main line is of course alive and well. The bay which most of the Hawkhurst trains started from was for some years used for van traffic, but by the early 1990's the former track bed had become part of a car park with the edge of the platform fenced off.

The former Hawkhurst branch bay at Paddock Wood Station which is now part of a car park. Note how the edge of the platform is fenced off. June 2nd 1991.   Author

29

The tile-hung former railway house at Churn Lane is now called "Churn Siding" but there is barely any other trace of the railway at this point.

The embankment through the valley at Swigs Hole and the cutting to the approach of Horsmonden Tunnel are still visible, while the tunnel under the B 2162 road is still there. However the very deep cutting on the Horsmonden side of the tunnel is fenced off to keep the public away from a dangerous drop.

The approach to Horsmonden Station has been partly filled in and the former station is now in use as a garage, appropriately called "Old Station Garage". The stationmaster's house, which faces the road, is still in use as a private dwelling - "Station House". The plate girder bridge which crossed the road has long gone and not a great deal of the former route between here and the site of Goudhurst Station at Hope Mill remains. In fact Goudhurst Station has completely vanished and has been replaced by a fine private house, appropriately called "Haltwhistle", built on what was part of the goods yard. It is surrounded by high conifer trees with a swimming pool built in between part of the former platforms. On the other side of the road from the level crossing the right of way is heavily overgrown. Where it was noted in the description of the route that the unsuspecting motorist driving over the level crossing when the station was in use could easily be mistaken in thinking that it might have been a main line with two tracks (one being the passing loop), the motorist today would never know that a railway once crossed the road at this point.

Between the site of Goudhurst Station and Pattenden Siding the three road bridges are still there, although the parapets have been removed on the second and third. The heavily overgrown right-of-way can just about be made out from the former level crossing to the second bridge, even though many small trees have grown up in the cutting. Some parts are filled in and others are like quicksand. From the site of the second to the third bridge, the route has completely disappeared. Very little remains at the site of Pattenden Siding to remind anyone of its past, although from here parts of the right-of-way have been reclaimed. Small sections can still be made out, and traces of cuttings and embankments can be seen in the woods before reaching the former Cranbrook Station at Hartley.

The former station building was for a time used as a pottery and what was the stationmaster's house is now a private dwelling, but has had a wing added to it, plus other alterations. The former goods shed still survives, as does part of the former goods yard both of which at the time of writing were in use as a "Gas Distribution Centre".

One encouraging thing about the remains of Cranbrook Station is that some of the platform railings and the running-in board were salvaged and transferred to Wittersham Road Station, on the preserved section of the Kent & East Sussex Railway.

The deep cuttings between Cranbrook Station and Badgers Oak Tunnel are heavily overgrown and a small stream seems to have settled into the trackbed of the former railway.

The plate girder bridge to the approach of Hawkhurst Station at Gills Green has been removed and the station site is now a wood turnery yard. The station building has been demolished but some remains of the platform and the overgrown site of the buffers can still be seen. The signal box is still there, in Southern Railway colours, with the name Hawkhurst in green and white.

The goods and locomotive sheds still survive and are used by the wood turnery company. Anyone entering the wood yard by footpath from the main road is still confronted by a green cast iron notice board which reads: "SOUTHERN RAILWAY CO. NOTICE IS HEREBY GIVEN IN PURSUANCE OF SECTION 90 OF THE SOUTHERN RAILWAY ACT, 1924, THAT THIS PATH IS A PRIVATE PATH. BY ORDER".

The former stationmaster's house, which is situated next to the former elevated station, is now a private dwelling, appropriately called "Old Station House".

Conclusion

During its whole existence, the Hawkhurst branch kept its original character right up until the last train, maintaining what is now the lost charm of our rural railways. If the proposed link-up between Cranbrook and Tenterden had been built, it is quite possible that at least part of the Paddock Wood to Hawkhurst line might have survived because, like its neighbour, the Kent & East Sussex Railway, if ever a railway called out for preservation it was the Hawkhurst branch.

Looking back, it is easy to remember all the good things and forget that this was one of the most steeply graded railways in the South of England, and that it left its passengers (with the exception of one station) between one and two miles from the town or village it claimed to serve. This said, it still managed to serve farmers and hop-growers and gave its passengers a journey through some of the most beautiful scenery that is everyone's image of Kent.

One personal memory that the author will never forget was, as a child, to stand at a point on the edge of Goudhurst village during the early evening and to see the glow of the train's engine entering the Teise Valley from Horsmonden, run along to Goudhurst Station and then on to Pattenden Siding and out of sight on its way towards Cranbrook.

Today the countryside in the area is as prosperous looking and as lovely as it ever was and is well worth a visit for this reason alone. But for the sentimental railway enthusiast it seems such a shame that maps of the district show parts of the route of the line as "site of railway (disused)", and the more up-to-date maps show no sign of the former railway at all.

The Hawkhurst branch line has now passed into history. It will be remembered with much affection by older local people and railway historians alike.

C class 0-6-0 No.31592 pulls an up goods train through Horsmonden Station. May 2nd 1961.

S.C.Nash

Acknowledgements

I would like to thank the following people and organisations for their kind help in compiling information and supplying photographs for this publication: Mr.R.F.Roberts, Mr.S.C.Nash, Mr.J.J.Smith, Mr.R.C.Riley, Mr.A.A.Jackson, Mr.B.R.Hart, Mr.A.E.Bennett, Mr.R.M.Casserley (for the H.C.Casserley photographs), Mr.J.H.Meredith, Mr.H.B.Priestley, Mr.G.Batchelor, Mr.D.Cullum, Mr.N.F.Rowe, Mr.G.Jacobs, Mr.H.Davies, Mr.K.G.Carr, Pamlin Prints, Mr.H.C.Bassett, Mr.G.R.Croughton, the Col. Stephens Railway Museum (Tenterden), the National Railway Museum (York), the librarians and staff of the reference libraries at Tunbridge Wells, Maidstone, Cranbrook and Ashford, the Public Records Office at Kew, and last but not least Mr.J.L.Smith of Lens of Sutton.

My thanks to my son Paul for reading my text and also to James Christian of Binfield Printers Ltd.

Bibliography

FORGOTTEN RAILWAYS: SOUTH-EAST ENGLAND by H.P.White (David & Charles)
THE RAILWAYS OF SOUTHERN ENGLAND: SECONDARY AND BRANCH LINES by Edwin Course (Batsford)
THE COLONEL STEPHENS RAILWAYS by John Scott-Morgan (David & Charles)
AN INTRODUCTION TO THE RAILWAYS OF PADDOCK WOOD by L.A.Summer (Published privately)
THE HAWKHURST RAILWAY by R. Crombleholme (Narrow Gauge & Light Railway Society)
BRANCH LINE TO HAWKHURST by Vic Mitchell and Keith Smith (Middleton Press)
THE ROTHER VALLEY, LATER THE KENT & EAST SUSSEX RAILWAY by M.Lawson Finch (Published privately)
SOUTH EASTERN RAILWAY by Adrian Gray (Middleton Press)
SOUTHERN RAILWAY BRANCH LINES IN THE THIRTIES by R.W.Kidner (Oakwood Press)
SOUTHERN RAILWAY BRANCH LINE TRAINS by R.W.Kidner (Oakwood Press)
SOUTHERN BRANCH LINES 1955 - 1965 by C.J.Gammell (Oxford Publishing)
RAILWAY MAGAZINE (Various issues)
TRAINS ILLUSTRATED (Various issues)

Cranbrook Station, after the track had just been removed. April 25th 1964.   R.C.Riley